By Alan Hardy & Peter Lorimer

Where is the horse gone?
Where the rider?
Where the giver of treasure?
Where are the seats at the feast?
Where are the revels in the hall?
Alas for the bright cup!
Alas for the mailed warrior!
Alas for the splendour of the prince!
How that time has passed away,
dark under the cover of night,
as if it had never been!

Lament from 'The Wanderer'
(10th century)

Today the town of ***Higham Ferrers*** spreads along high ground on the east bank of the River Nene, some 15 miles downstream from the county town, Northampton. A community of some 6000 people, the town's fine buildings and large ornate church testify to the historic importance of the town in the Middle Ages.

But what gave Higham Ferrers its importance? How did the town originate, and are there clues in its past to explain its later importance? Until now history could shed no light on the Dark Ages of Higham Ferrers. But in nine years of work spanning the turn of the 21st century, archaeologists have excavated a huge area on the outskirts of the town, revealing a wealth of evidence that illuminates those unknown times, telling a story both fascinating and intriguing, gruesome and tragic. Now, for the first time, the archaeology and history are brought together to throw light on the origins of Higham Ferrers. This book shows how, near the ruins of a Roman town, the early Anglo-Saxons came - bringing their own culture and beliefs from their ancestral homes in Europe - and formed the community that would in time be known as 'High Ham'.

The archaeological discoveries have shown that in later years Higham became part of a Saxon Royal Estate, part of Offa's great kingdom of Mercia. Higham was a centre for the collection of tributes and taxes, and, more darkly, a centre for trial and execution. The discoveries at Higham represent evidence of one of the earliest examples of Saxon government in action, the first in a line stretching all the way to today's Parliament.

Other discoveries show how the town has been affected by the Vikings, by medieval industry, politics and competition from its neighbours - in good times and bad - until today it has come full circle. Just as the early Saxons settled on the ridge overlooking the River Nene, so after 1500 years their descendants have returned to live there again.

But Why Dig Here...

In the early 1990s the Duchy of Lancaster - who have owned the land since the 13th century - began to sell off the area around Kings Meadow Lane - on the northern outskirts of Higham Ferrers - for the development of new housing. At that time the area was open fields, and aerial photographs and fieldwalking showed that traces of something important lay under the surface. Not only was there a Roman town (known about for some years previously), but there seemed to be an unusual form of Saxon settlement. Because of planning regulations, before the builders could move in, the archaeologists had time to excavate the areas that were going to be built on, to explore the archaeological evidence.

Who paid for it all?

A dig on this scale is a very expensive process, and the planning regulations required that the Duchy of Lancaster pay the cost - not only of the digging, but also of the analysis of all the evidence, and the production of the final report.
After all, there's no point in digging up all this evidence if you don't tell people about it afterwards!

Why not leave the excavated walls and ditches uncovered for people to see?

If a site like Kings Meadow Lane was left uncovered, it would be smothered in weeds and undergrowth in a short time, and the ditches and postholes would fill in with soil and rubbish - it would soon be a wilderness. To keep it looking at its best would cost many thousands of pounds each year. On top of that, the developer would rightly deserve some compensation for the houses he could no longer build!
Archaeologists must always balance the value of the past with the needs of the present - and remember, if it was not for the Duchy's development plans, and their enthusiastic support of the project, this story of Higham Ferrers could never be told!

The Romans...

By the middle of the 4th century AD, Britain - or Britannia as the Romans called it - had been a Roman province for more than 300 years. It was a well ordered and regulated society that in many ways operated like our own today. There were many towns - large and small - interconnected by a network of roads. People bought and sold goods and services with money, and there were public officials to help run the whole system. If you were rich, you would show off your

wealth by constructing grand buildings of stone or becoming a high official. Most people were civilians - that is, they left their security in the hands of a separate military force, namely the Roman Army. In return for that security, they paid taxes. It all sounds very familiar to us in the 21st century!

The Kings Meadow Lane excavations uncovered a large part of the Roman town, including the remains of 18 stone buildings, mostly along one side of a well-made road. On the other side of the road, overlooking the river, was a shrine where votive offerings were left to the Roman gods. Nearby was the remains of a massive stone platform that may have carried statues of those gods. Later on a new temple was built further along the road - from the fragments of stone columns recovered it must have been a grand building.

Behind the roadside buildings was a whole network of small fields and paddocks, and even a small cemetery along a lane leading up a shallow valley.

This was a thriving town - it's not too difficult for us imagine day-to-day life there, with traders and craftsmen selling their skills and wares to passers-by and visitors to the shrines.

Why it declined at the end of the 4th century is a story yet to be told, but the archaeology shows quite clearly that long before the first new settlers arrived, it was a town of ghosts, not people.

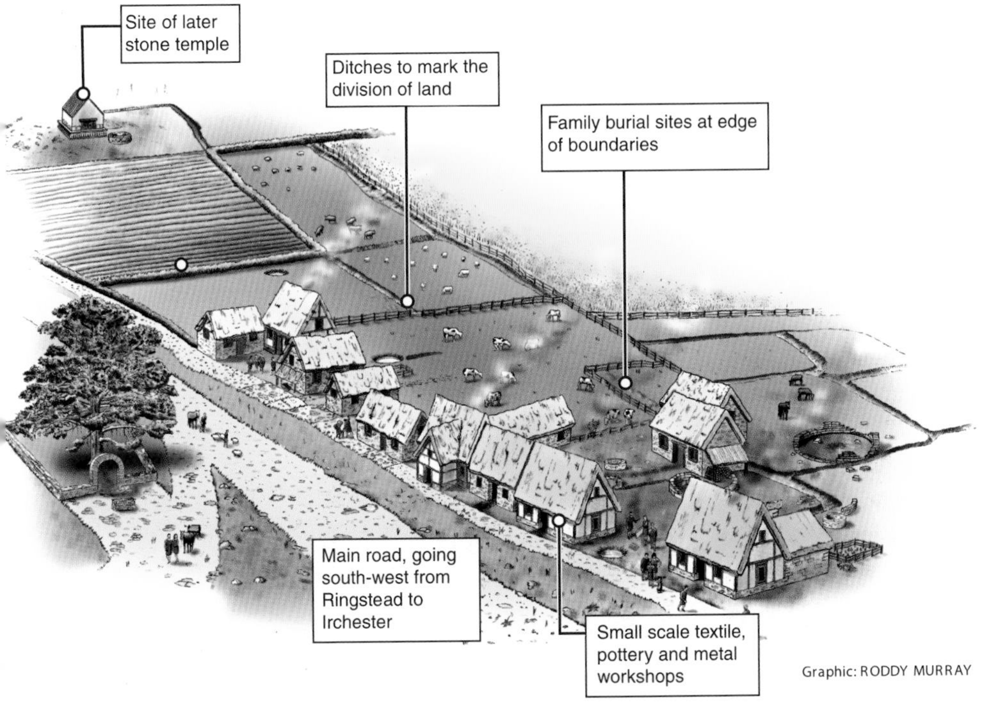

The end of the Romans

In the last decades of the 4th century, the once great Roman Empire at last began to collapse; it could no longer protect its own borders, and was being torn apart by civil wars. Rival emperors fought each other, while barbarian tribes hovered like vultures, waiting for the moment to strike. Rome had no

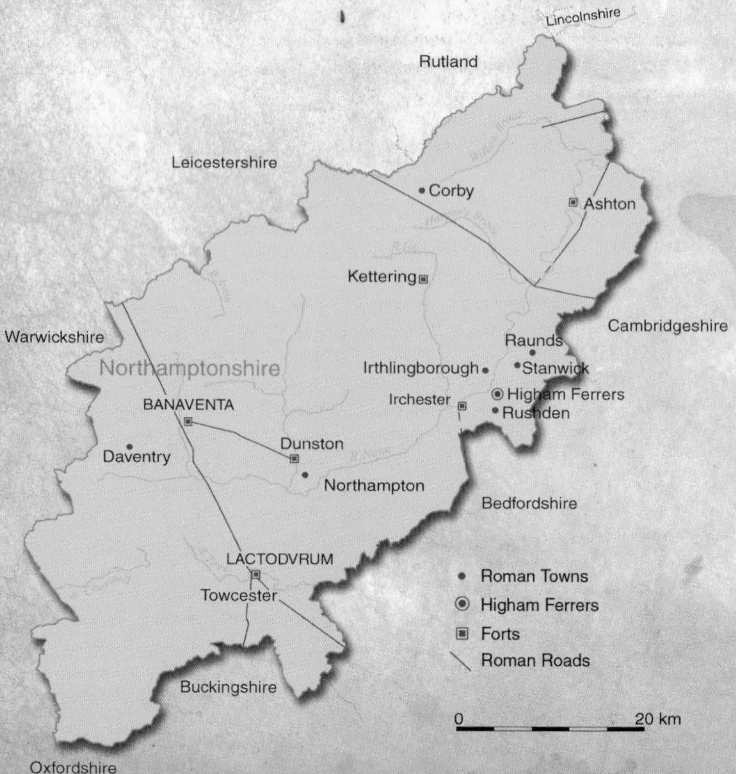

Lincolnshire
Rutland
Leicestershire
Corby
Ashton
Kettering
Cambridgeshire
Warwickshire
Northamptonshire
Raunds
Irthlingborough
Stanwick
Irchester
Higham Ferrers
Rushden
BANAVENTA
Daventry
Dunston
Northampton
Bedfordshire
LACTODVRUM
Towcester
Buckingshire
Oxfordshire

- Roman Towns
- Higham Ferrers
- Forts
- Roman Roads

0 20 km

choice - in a desperate attempt to survive, the Roman emperors began to withdraw from the farthest provinces, hoping that this would buy some breathing space.

Britannia had been suffering attacks from the Picts, from north of Hadrian's Wall, and from raiding Saxons from across the North Sea. When they heard that the Roman legions were leaving, the Britons sent a desperate plea for help to Emperor Honorius in AD 410. One historian recorded his answer - and it was not the message the Britons wanted to hear…

'Honorius dealt with the states of Britain by letter, telling them to look to their own defence……and remained inactive'

What happened next is still debated. In this book, we present one interpretation that seems to fit best with the evidence from Higham Ferrers.

At first the Britons succeeded in holding off the raiders, but they took a terrible risk to do so. They invited some of the Saxon raiders to change sides and become mercenaries, with promises of land and riches as rewards. This worked for a while, until the mercenaries realised their own power and increased their demands. Eventually civil war broke out, and for decades the Britons fought a desperate but losing fight against the Saxons.

Many myths emerged from this dark and troubled time, and one of the most powerful was that of Arthur, the gallant but doomed King of the Britons. Although the story that we know was not written down until the 13th century, most experts agree that the character of Arthur was based upon a real person, maybe one called Ambrosius, the vson of a high Roman official, who tried to rally the demoralised Britons to resist the Saxons. All the while, further groups of immigrants were crossing into eastern England, heading up the river valleys - like the Nene - and forming new communities....

The Early Saxons in Higham...

Unlike in some other parts of the country, by the time the first new settlers arrived - sometime in the middle of the 5th century - the Roman town had been derelict for a generation or more.

How did the incomers feel about what lay before them on the banks of the River Nene - an overgrown mess of dilapidated and ruined buildings, alongside a weed covered road?

It's likely that they took less notice than we might imagine. The river crossing point and the trackway leading up from it through the good quality land were important attractions, but they had no use for the ruined stone buildings or cobbled yards, or the scatter of Roman objects lying around. They ignored the old arrangement of fields and paddocks - there was plenty of room for everybody. The newcomers built their houses and arranged their new lives in the ways they were used to - why should they change?

Archaeology and the Anglo-Saxons

Trying to understand the Anglo-Saxons from the objects they left behind is very difficult. The Romans built in stone, made many metal objects - including coins - and hard, long-lasting pottery, all things that survive well in the ground, and can be dated, sometimes very accurately. The Anglo-Saxons almost always built in wood, made fewer metal objects (and sometimes no coins at all) and their pottery was much more fragile. It is therefore much more difficult to work out from the remains what was happening - and when it was happening.

Only in the Anglo-Saxon cemeteries, and particularly their pre-Christian cemeteries, can we find lots of objects, buried with the bodies, to give clues about their lives. The trouble is, at Kings Meadow Lane we did not find a cemetery - in early Anglo-Saxon times they were usually some distance from the settlement. So we are left with the evidence from their everyday life.

Among their day-to-day rubbish, thrown away in pits, were objects made of bone, some useful, others decorative. A group of nine bone needles were found together - they must have been linked together by a leather thong through each of the eyes - which may have been used for mending fishing nets. Fragments of very delicate decorated bone combs were found,

which seem to have been used not only for combing hair, but as decoration or a sign of status.

We found fragile black pottery, made without a wheel, and some pieces of a type of pottery that was made in Ipswich, so we know they traded into East Anglia. Many bones of cattle, pigs and sheep were found, some of them showing knife marks where they were butchered - telling us that domestic farm animals were very important as a food resource to them.

When all the finds have been cleaned and marked, analysed and in some cases photographed, they will be stored in the County Museum - for future researchers to study. A few will find their way into Museum displays.

Early Saxon buildings

Each building consisted of a rectangular flat-bottomed pit about 3 metres long by 2 metres wide, and up to half a metre deep. At each end of the pit was a large post, supporting a suspended wooden floor. The pit served as a cool storage place, perhaps for food. Some houses look as though the base of the pit itself was the house floor. These houses are called Sunken Featured Buildings - or SFBs - by archaeologists, and some of them, reconstructed from the archaeological evidence, can be seen today at West Stow near Bury St Edmunds.

An SFB would have lasted about 20 years. When the posts had rotted through, a new building would be constructed nearby, and the pit of the old one would be used for rubbish. Because of these buildings, we have learnt much about the early Anglo-Saxon way of life, because the SFB pit is often full of pottery and animal bone, and some of their trinkets.

A total of ten such buildings were found on the whole site, either standing alone or in groups of two or three. It seems likely that only three or four were standing at any one time. so we might imagine that maybe two or three families settled on the high ground near to the ruined town, and later slowly spread away from the river, each family claiming and clearing their own patch of land to live on, tend their animals and cultivate their crops. The houses were not grouped together in the form of a village as we would understand it, but all the settlers would have thought of themselves as members of a people or tribe.

Anglo-Saxon society

from kinship to kingship

Anglo-Saxon society was very different from Roman ways of living. The few Anglo-Saxon families who settled at Higham had a very different outlook on life and the world around them. They were not used to living in large and complex towns, and had no interest in the elaborate Roman society - to them 'kinship' was at the heart of everything.

Kinship was all about personal loyalty to your family and relatives ('kin') above everything else. In the early days you would not know many other people anyway, so it worked well. Slowly these family groups grew into tribes, but the idea of kinship remained. You depended on your kin for support, and were responsible for them if they did wrong. One of the worst punishments was to banish someone - they would then be alone, a stranger without kin wherever they went.

The word 'king' comes from the Saxon ***cyning,*** and meant somebody from a kin group chosen to be leader. The early Anglo-Saxon tribal leaders acquired their power from their ability as warriors. They evolved into kings, each supported by a loyal band of armed men, every one utterly devoted to his leader. In return for their support they received gifts of plunder and the king's protection.

It was important for a king to display his power wherever he went. Bede wrote of one of the Northumbrian Kings:

'Truly he kept such great state in his kingdom, that not only were his banners borne before him in war, but even in time of peace his standard bearer always went before him as he rode between his residences and provinces with his thegns* [warriors]*.'

As the role of kingship developed, so the duties did too. A king had to be active and involved in his kingdom -

'In the winter and the spring the king used to travel through all the provinces....and enquire diligently whether the laws of the land and his own ordinances [orders] were obeyed, so that the poor might not suffer wrong and be oppressed by the powerful. Thus his enemies on every side were filled with awe, and the love of those who owed him allegiance was secured.'

Our sources

In contrast to the Romans, who had a long tradition of recording everything in writing, the early Saxons' culture relied upon the spoken word. There is very little recorded history of the early Anglo-Saxon period in England, and none that is certainly based on eyewitness accounts. When the story of an event is passed down from memory, it can rapidly change and become distorted
The two most important writers of the times were Gildas and Bede.

Gildas 500 - 570

Gildas was born in the Strathclyde or Cwm Cawlwyd area around AD 500. He was well educated for his time, and is remembered for his piece called *The Ruin of Britain* in which he described the coming of the Saxons and the terrible fate that befell the Britons, when the Romano-British princes failed to resist and defend their land.

More a sermon than an objective history, he relied upon the memories of still living men for the course of events in the 5th century.

Bede 673-735

Born near Newcastle-on-Tyne, he became a monk at the twin monastery of Monkwearmouth-Jarrow. Most of his writings were studies on the Bible, but his most important work in historians' eyes was *The ecclesiastical history of the English people,* written around the year 731, and the first attempt to write a national history. However, he focused on the coming of Christianity in AD 597, and only sketchily described events before that date. Also, his account of events after that date was written from the point of view of Northumbria, where he lived. His work contains little detail about Mercia, for instance.

The Anglo Saxon Chronicle

This is a modern name for a collection of writings - by various authors - first put together on the orders of King Alfred in the late 9th century. It was an attempt to chart the history of the country, from the Roman conquest in AD 43 onwards, and create an image of the slow evolution of the English nation, culminating in the heroic struggle of Alfred against the Danes. Alfred wanted the Chronicle to give a sense of identity and confidence to the hard pressed English. While in general it seems quite accurate, the precise dates - especially of the early years - are unreliable, and the whole Chronicle is written from the point of view of the Kingdom of Wessex.

In later years many of the copies had additional sections added to them, right up to the 11th century.

Other documents

From the 7th century onwards, as the new Saxon kingdoms grew and made laws for the regulation of society, so did the need to write things down - the detail of laws, records of who owned what piece of land, charters confirming gifts of land to churches, charters confirming the King's authority, and so on. Many of these documents survive, and they have helped to tell us something of the way Anglo-Saxon society was run at the time.

The new Christian Church put great store by reading and writing, and were past masters at meticulous record keeping.

The Tribute Centre...

The complex of buildings and ditches that were built in the later part of the 7th century were very unusual. The most spectacular part was a huge open space, surrounded by a ditch - forming a horseshoe-shaped enclosure. This was no ordinary field or paddock - it was nearly as big as a football pitch. No trace of a building, or any sign of human activity was found within the enclosure.

Across the open end of the enclosure was a fence and a number of long buildings ('halls'). A short while later two straight ditches were added, leading from the tips of the horseshoe to the south, forming a big wide funnel leading from Kings Meadow Lane up to the enclosure. More halls were built in this funnel area.

The whole complex was clearly very carefully planned and laid out. It is far too big and too spread out to be a single farm, and the objects found in the ditches and all over the site do not look as though they belonged to particularly wealthy people. It does not seem to be a village, as there are almost no rubbish pits and little sign of the normal activities that would be going on in a village, such as spinning or weaving.

Site 2
Site 3
Site 8
Site 6
Site 7
Windmill Banks
Kings Avenue
North End

And although there are many buildings, only two contained a hearth or fireplace - a sign that they were occupied.

There is one site, at Yeavering, in Northumberland, where there is a similar huge enclosure and a series of buildings, and a similar lack of evidence of everyday life. It was dug in the 1950s and both the dig and documentary evidence show that it was a Royal centre for the Northumbrian kings in the 7th century. The huge enclosure was - like the one at Higham - empty of any building and has been interpreted as a huge enclosure to accept cattle or other stock as tributes to the king. In this case, however, the king's hall and other royal buildings were right beside the corral. At Higham there are large buildings, but most of them appear to be more like storehouses than palaces. So it seems that Yeavering might explain part of the evidence - but we may have to look across the river to Irthlingborough for the rest of the story.

Enough documentary evidence survives to show that in the 8th century Irthlingborough was a Royal centre, and at least one charter survives that was signed there - sometime between 787 and 796 - by Offa, King of Mercia. In the charter he confirmed the gift of some land by Oslac, ruler of the South Saxons, to the church of St Paul in Earnley, Sussex.

Every Royal centre had its tribute centre, and it would have made sense for the tribute centre or ***feorm*** (from which we get 'farm') of Irthlingborough to be close by. By situating it across the river, it was a statement saying 'The King controls both north and south of the river, and the river itself'. The big enclosure at Higham was visible from Irthlingborough, and to get from one to the other would have been fairly easy as the river was wide but shallow.

Higham was not the only Anglo-Saxon settlement in the region. The land was good for farming, and easy to reach for the new settlers coming in from the east. All along both banks of the River Nene, many traces of settlement have been found, such as at Raunds where evidence has been found of a well-planned manor, which later included a church and graveyard.

What's in a name?

Sometimes the name of a modern town or village can tell us that it had a Saxon beginning. 'Ham' is a Saxon word meaning an important enclosure, so Higham is 'the important enclosure on the hill'.

The original spelling of Irthlingborough was Yrtlinga burg. The "-inga-" part seems to be common among places set up by colonising settlers in the 7th century, and "-burg" is Anglo-Saxon for a fortification - sometimes a prehistoric one. So Irthlingborough is 'The new settlement in the old fort' - perhaps "Yrtl" was the name of the original settler!

You are what you.... Grow?

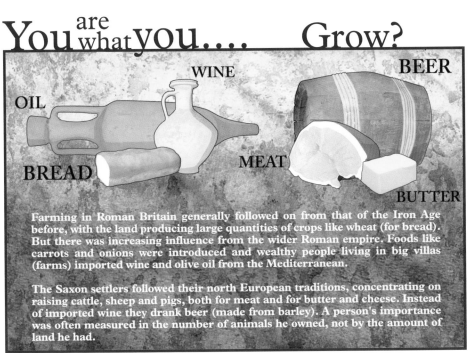

WINE BEER

OIL

BREAD MEAT

BUTTER

Farming in Roman Britain generally followed on from that of the Iron Age before, with the land producing large quantities of crops like wheat (for bread). But there was increasing influence from the wider Roman empire. Foods like carrots and onions were introduced and wealthy people living in big villas (farms) imported wine and olive oil from the Mediterranean.

The Saxon settlers followed their north European traditions, concentrating on raising cattle, sheep and pigs, both for meat and for butter and cheese. Instead of imported wine they drank beer (made from barley). A person's importance was often measured in the number of animals he owned, not by the amount of land he had.

What was a tribute centre for?

As the Anglo-Saxon kingdoms grew more powerful and complex, their kings could no longer rely upon accepting gifts or taking plunder in raids as a way of maintaining their power. They had to develop a way of supporting their power by means of regular tributes - taxes - from their subjects. Unlike the Romans, the Anglo-Saxons did not have a system based upon money, so tributes would have to be paid in kind, that is, in the different sorts of things his subjects were producing. As an Anglo-Saxon subject the amount you paid in tribute every year was fixed by the King, and depended on the amount of land you had. This is one yearly requirement from ten hides of land in the 8th century:

"ten vats of honey, 300 loaves, twelve ambers of Welsh ale, thirty of clear ale, two full grown cows or ten wethers (calves), ten geese, twenty hens, ten cheeses, an amber (barrel) full of butter, five salmon, twenty pounds of fodder (hay) and 100 eels"

THE SPECIALIST'S REPORT

Emma-Jayne Evans *Animal Bone Specialist*

Animal bones - part of the rubbish of everyday life - are often found in many of the ditches and pits. By identifying the species and age of the animals, we can see what animals were kept at the tribute centre. We can see how well people looked after their animals, and at what age they were killed. If the animals were old when they died, this can mean they were used for milk, wool or for as beasts of burden, not just for meat.

The bones found around the tribute centre show how the importance of different animals changed over time, as shown on the chart below. There is a clear change in the numbers of animals kept when the big stock pen was abandoned - suddenly there's a lot fewer pigs and sheep. This shows that the stock pen may have held pigs and sheep as well as cattle.

Much later - in the 14th and 15th centuries - the proportion of sheep increases sharply - this is typical of the time when sheep-farming became very popular and profitable.

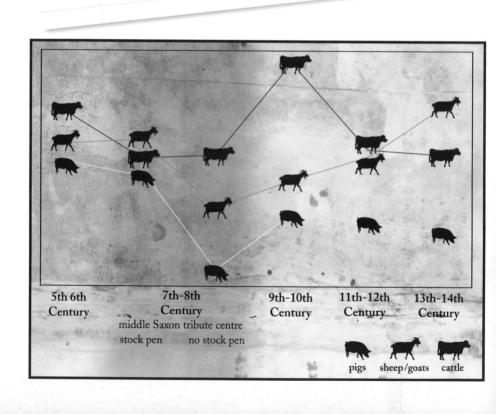

5th 6th Century

7th-8th Century

middle Saxon tribute centre

stock pen — no stock pen

9th-10th Century

11th-12th Century

13th-14th Century

pigs — sheep/goats — cattle

By looking at the physical evidence of the tribute centre, we can work out what kinds of products were considered important enough to be demanded by the king.

How was a tribute paid?

In charge of the collecting would be a representative of the King, called a ***reeve or gerefa.*** He would have a record of who had to pay what, and at a certain times of the year - when the King was in residence, or at harvest time - he would command that all those living in the region should bring their tribute to the estate centre. Failure to do so, or attempts to cheat, were very serious crimes, sometimes punishable by death. Whatever was brought in was stored temporarily, either in the enclosure - in the case of animals - or in the many storehouses and barns. Later it was sent on elsewhere, or eaten or used in the Royal centre, and so there are few traces for us to find.

The tribute centre buildings

At least seven different buildings were discovered in the tribute centre. Some of these were very simple in layout and probably served as storage barns for all the produce brought in tribute. As the Anglo-Saxons did not use stone in their houses, the only evidence that survives to show that a building

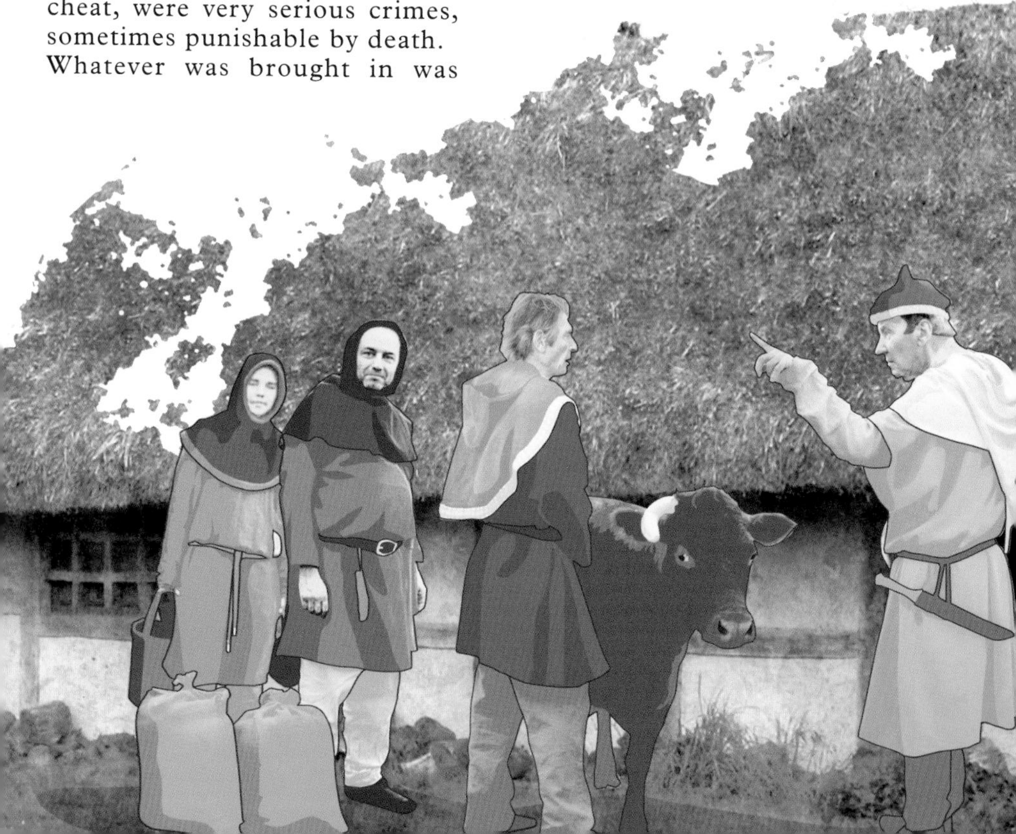

existed is the holes dug into the ground to hold upright posts that formed the framework of the walls.

What did the buildings look like?

The buildings were usually rectangular - anything from 10 to 25 metres long and as much as 7 metres wide. The gaps between the wall posts would have been filled with plaster coated onto a web of thin twigs or withies, forming weatherproof walls. The roof was most likely made of thatch. In the buildings that were lived in, the fireplace would be a simple open hearth. There was no need for a chimney - the smoke from a fire would find its way out through the thatch.

One of the buildings was clearly much more than just a barn. It was the most elaborate in layout, and was probably the important hall where the ***reeve*** or ***gerefa*** lived. At one end there was a dividing wall - maybe this screened off a private chamber from the main hall. The shallow trench running down the centre of the main room would have held a long plank, and this would have supported upright wooden supports. This tells us that there was either an upper floor or a least a storage area in the roof over the main room.

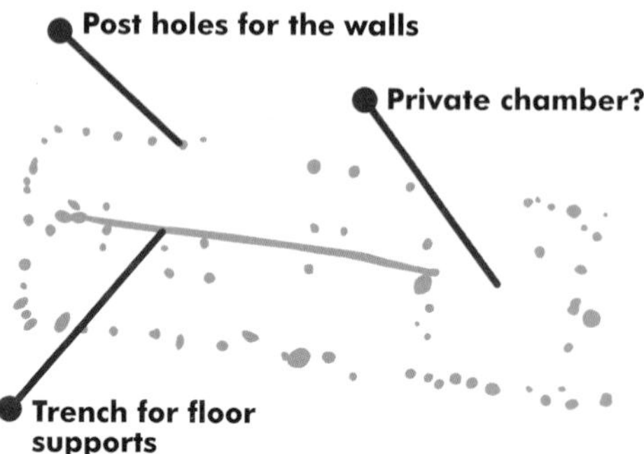

Windows would be simple openings protected by wooden shutters - window glass would only be used later in churches. Light would be provided by tallow (animal fat) lamps, casting a low, warm light round the room. Here the business of the Tribute Centre would be conducted, and feasts for the ***gerefa*** and his guests would be held.

Anglo-Saxon culture

Although Anglo-Saxon society officially adopted Christianity by the 8th century, their culture, based around kinship, or the family, and rooted in the veneration of their warrior ancestors persisted, and the great sagas and poems - stirring tales of the heroes of the past - continued to be told and retold, and eventually written down.

Central to that culture was the hall, in which great gatherings of the kin would take place with the telling of stories and the singing of songs, all accompanied by the drinking of beer.

In such an atmosphere the heroic stories of their ancestors would be told - stories such as Beowulf, the adventures of a great warrior king of the past.

'There was hurry and hest in Heorot now
for hands to bedeck it, and dense was the throng
of men and women the wine-hall to cleanse,
the guest-room to garnish. Gold-gay shone the hangings
that were wove on the wall, and wonders many to delight each mortal that looks upon them'.

'Ða wæs haten hreþe Heort innanweard
folmum gefrætwod. Fela þæra wæs,
wera ond wifa, þe þæt winreced,
gestsele gyredon. Goldfag scinon
web æfter wagum, wundorsiona fela
secga gehwylcum þara þe on swylc starað'.

In Beowulf, and in many other poems that have survived for us to read, these stories have a strong sense of sadness and nostalgia, as if the teller wished that he could live the uncomplicated and exciting life of a warrior again, instead of being a farmer in an ever safer, but ever more unexciting society!

THE MALTING OVEN

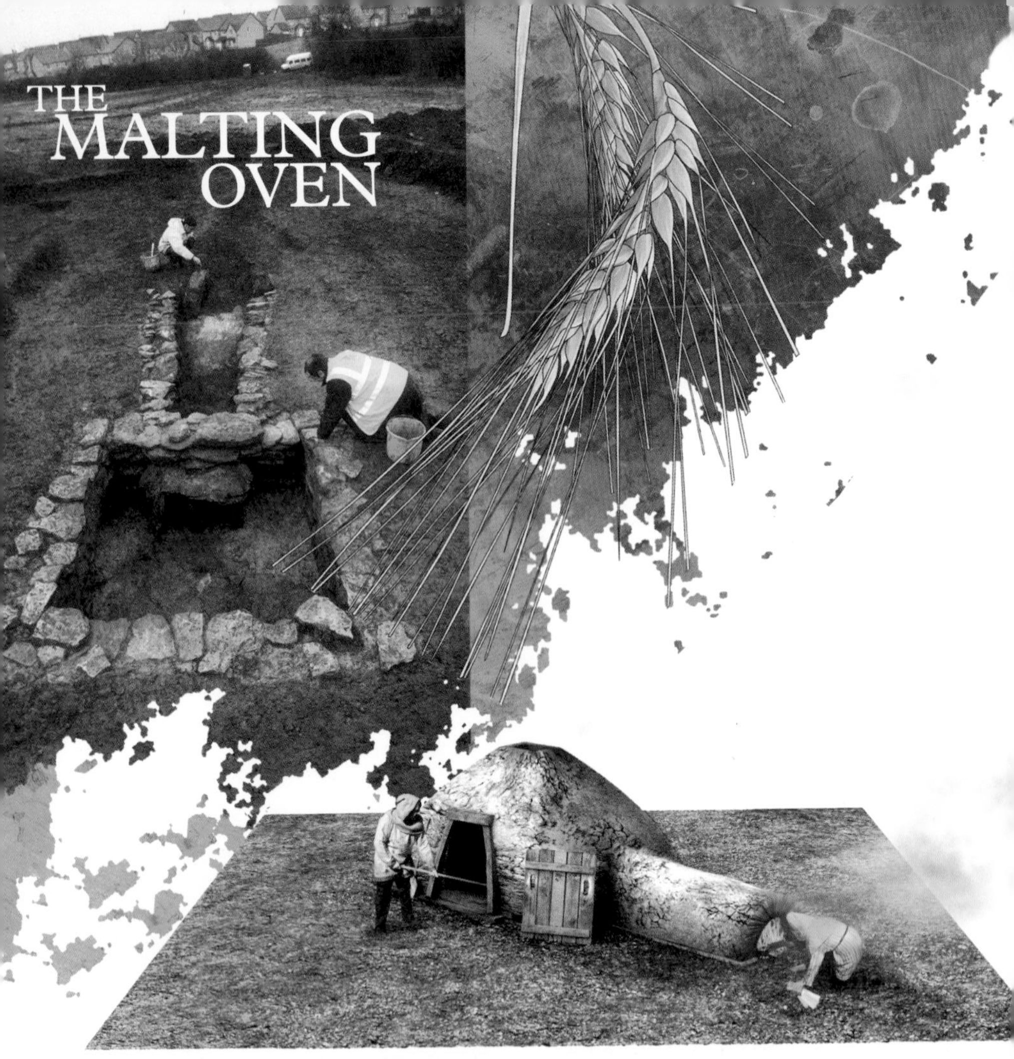

One building, found on the other side of the Lane, tells us a lot about how the Saxons entertained themselves. As the Romans prized their wine, so the Anglo-Saxons loved their beer, and we had discovered a malting oven. It was set well away from other buildings, to reduce the fire risk (although there were probably sheds and temporary buildings nearby) and its base was built of stone with a sunken clay floor and a channel, or flue, extending out of one end. The stone sides probably only came up to ground level. When it was excavated the oven contained many pieces of fired clay. Some of the pieces had deep impressions of wattles (thin poles) in their surface, and others had flat surfaces where they had pressed against sawn pieces of wood.

HIGHAM FERRERS

From the pieces of the fired clay we have been able to show that a square timber frame rested on the stone base. The wattles were pegged into the wooden base, and their ends woven and tied together to form a tunnel shape, with a central chimney vent. The framework was plastered with a thick layer of clay, dug from a pit nearby. To make the clay hard and weatherproof, a fire was lit in the chamber and kept burning for a few days, and the oven floor and the sides of the stone walls still showed red where they had been exposed to the heat. Once the clay dome was fired, the malting of the grain could begin.

How did this oven work?

The germinating barley grain was spread out on sacking on a wooden platform suspended over the sunken floor, and a fire lit at the entrance to the flue. This would be kept burning for up to five days, the heat being drawn into the chamber and up through the layer of grain. Finally the oven would be opened and the malted grain removed for the next stage in the brewing process.

Why is this oven special?

Other ovens of this period found in this country have been small, crude structures, often re-used furnaces. Nothing of this size has been found before, and it must mean that it was purpose-built to process a lot of grain - the Royal centre over the river would have had a good supply of beer!

What is malting?

To make beer from grain, the barley is soaked in water for a day or two, and then spread out on a floor, where it begins to germinate, and the starch in the grain turns to sugar. The grain is then gently heated to about 60-100°C in an oven, which stops the germination. The malted grain is then milled to produce a grist, which is added to water, boiled, and sealed in casks. Honey can be added to sweeten the taste and produce mead.

The importance of beer

Beer was of central importance to their way of life, and not just as something to drink in place of water, which was not always clean. The Anglo-Saxons had a rich tradition of their warrior past, when leaders would join with their friends in the mead hall to feast and drink. Saxon literature, like the great saga of Beowulf, is littered with mentions of beer as a central part of the reinforcement of kinship and

THE SPECIALIST'S REPORT

Lisa Moffett *Charred Plant Remains Specialist*

More than half a kilo (nearly 2lb) of charred cereal grains were found on the floor of the oven, many of them sprouted - a sign they were being malted. Most of the grains were barley, although there were some oats and wheat as well. Barley was the best cereal for beer-making, but sometimes cereals were deliberately mixed to give a different flavour to the beer. On the other hand, in this case it could have been simply that some oats and wheat were growing among the barley crop.

Very few weed seeds or chaff (grain husks) were found, showing that great care was taken to clean the crops before the malting process began.

But if such care was taken, why was so much grain left behind? - it's possible that the last use of the oven ended in a accident - perhaps the roasting platform collapsed, spilling some of the roasted grain of the platform onto the oven floor!

friendship. The halls themselves were often referred to as beer halls or mead halls. Boasting was a favourite pastime among men, and the consumption of large quantities of beer undoubtedly helped! However, in contrast to some parts of our own modern culture, extreme drunkenness was discouraged. You could not be a warrior if you could not stand up!

Wealhtheow, Hrothgar's queen,
came forth, mindful of kin,
adorned in gold to greet the men.
First she gave the cup
to the country's guardian,
that one dear to his people,
biding joy in his beer drinking.
That king famous for victories
happily took the feast cup.
Then that woman of the Helmings
went round to each, young and old,
sharing the precious cup.

The Kingdom of Mercia

The kingdom of Mercia was one of three great powers that ruled England between the late 6th and 9th centuries. In the north was Northumbria - in the south and west was Wessex; each struggled to survive and dominate the other two. Mercia began as a loose grouping of many small tribes, and was originally centred around the West Midlands. As it grew in strength and territory, it spread to take in all central England, as far north as the Humber, as far west as the borders of modern Wales, and as far south as the Thames Valley. Under its greatest kings, Aethelbald and Offa, it became the strongest of the three kingdoms.
Higham lay in the territory of the Middle Angles, a mysterious and little known people, who we think came originally from northern Germany. The Middle Angles were under Mercian control, but were never completely absorbed, so that they kept their own 'sub-kings', who ruled in the name of the Mercian king.

The Tribal Hidage

A valuable document of this time is the *Tribal Hidage*, a register of the amount of land occupied by all the tribes in England. The earliest copy is dated from the 10th century, but the original is likely to date at least 200 years earlier. Some of the names are lost to us, some are mentioned nowhere else, but some are very familiar.

The land of the Mercians is 30,000 hides what is called the original Mercia. Wocen saetna is 7000 hides. Westerna the same. Pecsaena 1200 hides. Elmed saetna 600 hides, Lindes farona 7000 hides including haeth feld land. South gyrwa 600 hides North gyrwa 600 hides. East wixna 300 hides. West wixna 600 hides. Spalda 600 hides. Wigesta 900 hides. Herefinna 1200 hides. Sweord ora 300 hides. Gifla 300 hides. Hicca 300 hides. With gara 600 hides. Nox gaga 5000 hides. Oht gaga 2000 hides. That is 66,100 hides.
Hwinca 7000 hides. Chiltern saetna 4000 hides. Hendrica 3500 hides. Unecun gaga 1200 hides. Aro saetna 600 hides.
Faerpinga 300 hides. Bilmiga 600 hides. Widerigga the same. East willa 600 hides. West willa 600 hides. East angles 30,000 hides. East saxons 7000 hides. Cantarawena 15,000 hides.
South saxons 7000 hides. West saxons 100,000 hides. All of which is 242,700 hides.

What is a hide?

A 'hide' was a measure of land area in Saxon times. It represented that amount of land sufficient to support a single family, and so could measure different sizes depending on the quality of the land.

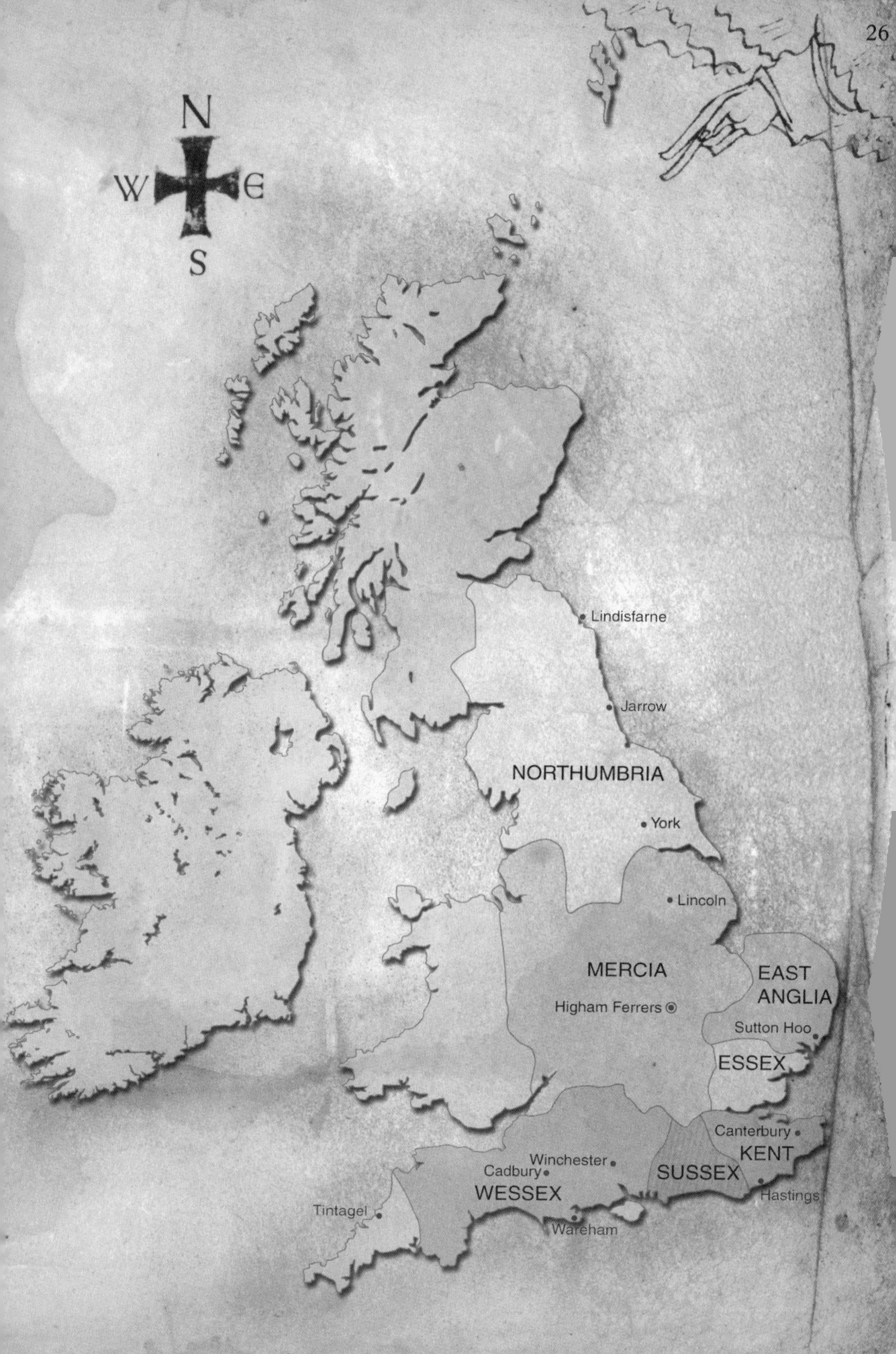
N
W
E
S
Lindisfarne
Jarrow
NORTHUMBRIA
York
Lincoln
MERCIA
EAST
ANGLIA
Higham Ferrers
Sutton Hoo
ESSEX
Canterbury
KENT
Winchester
Cadbury
SUSSEX
WESSEX
Hastings
Tintagel
Wareham

The greatest kings

Aethelbald (716-757)

Early in his reign he took advantage of the death of Wihtred, King of Kent, and departure of Ine, King of Wessex to Rome, to extend Mercian authority over the Middle Angles. He also controlled Wessex and London for a time, and launched attacks on Northumbria. He was one of the first kings to use the power of the church to reinforce his rule, but still suffered increasing resistance in his last years.

Offa (757-796)

Ambitious and energetic, and driven by a craving for power, Offa rebuilt the Mercian kingdom, and strengthened his influence in East Anglia and Essex. He ruled by reputation, and was a ruthless politician. Determined to secure the throne for his family, he consecrated his son as King in 787. Offa was influenced by what Charlemagne, King of the Franks, was doing in Northern France at the same time, and longed to create a similarly vast empire. But Offa did not have the time, the patience or the resources to achieve this goal. Offa's Dyke, designed as a barrier against the marauding Welsh, is the best reminder of his ambition.

The end of Mercia

By the middle of the 9th century, under pressure from the increasingly powerful kingdom of Wessex, and the growing threat from invading Vikings, Mercia weakened, eventually becoming a puppet state under Wessex's control.

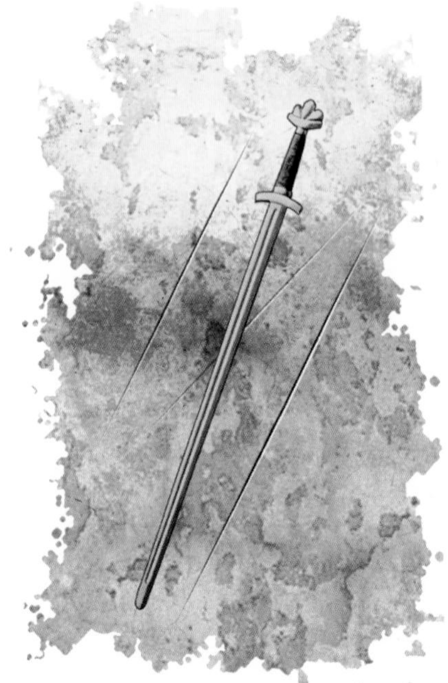

Christianity

When the Romans left, so did a lot of the support for Christianity over much of Britain. The newcomers were pagans and had their own array of gods, and it was not until late in the 6th century that the first missionaries, led by Augustine and sent by the Pope in Rome, landed in Kent. They set about converting the Anglo-Saxon kings - reasoning that where the king went, his people would follow. One of their first successes was with Ethelbert, King of Kent, who was a pagan married to a Christian princess from France. He allowed the missionaries to use an old Roman church in Canterbury and soon became a convert himself.

Other kings could see the attraction of converting and making use of the support the Church would give them in preserving their rule - and so one by one they accepted the new religion. It became important for an Anglo-Saxon king to show how he was descended from Woden. Having taken on Christianity, it was easy to add on the family trees from the Bible to take your ancestry right back to Adam!

Along with new ways of thinking on the subjects of kingship, the new Christianity meant new churches - and churches built of stone. Only now did the Anglo-Saxons take note of the Roman ruins still gently decaying around them, and many of the new churches were built from the stone of the old Roman ruins. In Northamptonshire two fine examples of late Saxon churches can be found at Earls Barton and Brixworth.

Although Christianity replaced the old ways, the names of Saxon (and one Roman) gods and goddesses are still preserved in our names for the days of the week

Monday : Moon day
Tuesday : Tiws day
Wednesday : Wodens day
Thursday : Thors day
Friday : Freyjas day
Saturday : Saturns day
Sunday : (literally) Sun day

THE STORY OF THE SPARROW

When King Edwin of Northumbria was considering whether to accept the new Christianity, one of his counsellors told this story:

'Your Majesty, when we compare the present life of man on earth with that time of which we have no knowledge, it seems to me like the swift flight of a single sparrow through the hall where you are sitting at dinner on a winter's day with your thegns and counsellors. In the midst there is a comforting fire to warm the hall; outside, the storms of winter rain or snow are raging. This sparrow flies swiftly in through one door of the hall, and out through another. While he is inside, he is safe from the winter storms; but after a few moments of comfort, he vanishes from sight into the wintry world from which he came. Even so, man appears on earth for a little while; but of what went before this life or of what follows, we know nothing. Therefore, if this new teaching has brought any more certain knowledge, it seems only right that we should follow it.'

In an uncertain and dangerous world, the apparent certainties of Christianity gave the Anglo-Saxon kings more confidence than their old beliefs.

The final years of the tribute centre

By the late 8th century the tribute centre had been changed again. The stock pen was abandoned and the horseshoe ditch allowed to fill in. In its place the straight ditch was extended across and then turned southwards along the line of the present main road.

Why was the big corral abandoned?

Maybe the tribute system was changed, so that there was no need to corral animals at the centre. Finally, at around the end of the 8th century, the big perimeter ditch was filled in. This seems to mean that there was a deliberate decision to close down the tribute centre. What could have been the reason? We think it must have been a political decision. Had the royal centre of Irthlingborough lost its role? It may be so - for Offa himself - the last great Mercian king, died in 796.

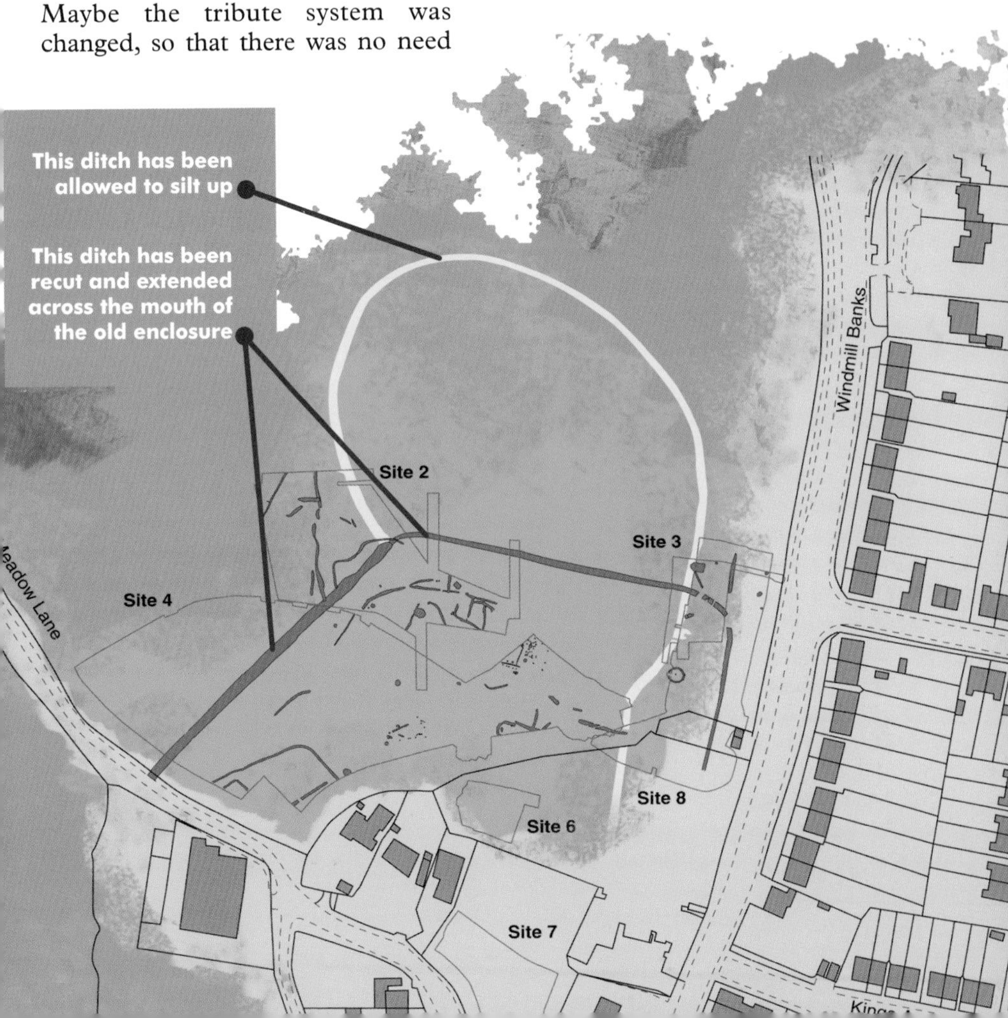

THE WOMAN IN THE DITCH

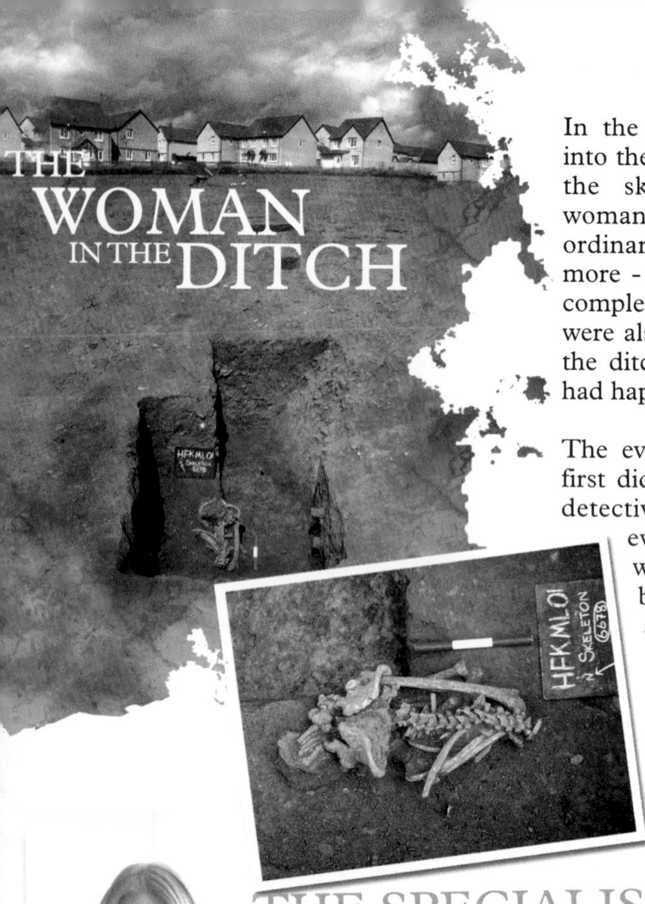

In the midst of the earth thrown into the ditch was a gruesome find - the skeleton of a middle-aged woman. But this was clearly no ordinary death..... And there was more - part of a leg bone, and two complete lower jaws of young men were also found at the same level in the ditch, a few metres away. What had happened here?

The evidence was unusual, and at first didn't make sense, but - like a detective story - bit by bit the evidence of the bones, and where they were found, have been fitted together to make a likely explanation.

Read on..

THE SPECIALIST'S REPORT

Annsofie Witkin *Human Bone Specialist*

The woman's body tells us much - her head and neck, and both arms were missing. Her legs were tightly folded up against her body, as though theywere bound, or maybe her remains had been put in a sack.

When the bones were analysed in the laboratory it was noticed that a vertebra - from the lower part of her back - was missing. There were tooth marks from a fox or small dog on two of the vertebrae - also from the lower back.

What had happened to this woman? She was almost certainly executed, probably by hanging. After death she was strung up by her legs. The arms and the head were likely to have been removed by scavenging animals In time, the rotting corpse separated at its weakest point, at the middle of the body, and the torso fell to the ground, where it was gnawed by animals. Eventually the remains were collected up and disposed of in the ditch.

All the body parts - from the woman and the men -were put into the ditch at the same time, just as the ditch was being filled in, but they died many years apart! The radiocarbon dates from the woman and one of the jaws gave a similar date - about the end of the 8th century. The other jaw gave adate many years earlier. How can we explain this?

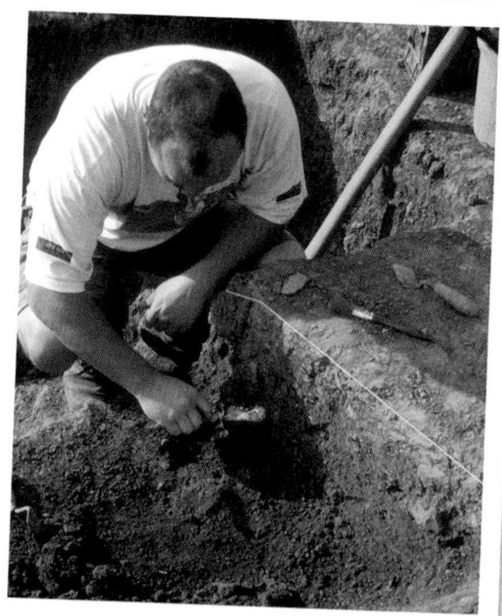

It seems that what we had found were the human remains from an execution site, which must have been close by, alongside the lane. Here, for many years, executions had taken place - probably by hanging - and the bodies left exposed, decaying and disintegrating, to act as a warning to other would-be criminals. Finally, when the tribute centre was abandoned, the execution site was cleared and the gruesome remains of the bodies - the woman was probably the most recent victim - were collected up in sacks and dumped in the ditch, which was then filled in.

Not only does this tell us a lot about the way criminal justice was carried out, but it is a reminder about the importance of the tribute centre. The execution site was close to the main road down to the river and across to the Royal site at Irthlingborough. Anyone travelling along the lane could not avoid seeing the execution site, the hanging, decaying bodies, and be reminded very clearly of the power and authority of the King.

The trial

It is most likely that - like the earlier victims - the woman stood trial before her execution. In some ways, her trial would have looked familiar to us, and many of the principles of trial by jury today originated in Saxon times. She would have taken an oath to tell the truth, in front of a 'jury' of important people - not ordinary citizens like today - these would be people of high rank or thegns led by the ***gerefa*** or ***reeve***, the representative of the King.

Crime and punishment in Anglo-Saxon England

What were these people's crimes that led to their awful end?
At this time, there was no single countrywide rule of law - each king would devise his own set of rules for keeping social order. As the country slowly began to settle into peace from the early Saxon tribal struggles, so each King needed a system of justice to maintain social stability. Laws tended to reflect the way people generally acted, and justice had two central aspects, compensation for the victim and punishment of the criminal.
A person's life had a legal value (***wergild***) dependent on his or her social status. A murderer, for instance, could 'pay' for his crime (literally) by paying his victim's ***wergild*** to the family or kin.

As far as punishment was concerned, the idea of imprisoning someone for a crime did not exist - there were no prisons.

What was the death penalty used for?

The death penalty applied to many offences, and it shows what was important to kings in Anglo-Saxon society. Conspiracy against the king - perhaps by colluding with another kingdom to overthrow the ruler - non-payment of rent, theft of the king's tribute, or minting coins without permission - all these were a threat to the king's fragile authority, and had to be met with harsh justice. Maybe the two men had been caught stealing the king's cattle from the enclosure. Maybe the woman had conspired with another king, or was she perhaps guilty of witchcraft?

Witchcraft

A crime which possibly involved women more than men was witchcraft. In the 7th and 8th centuries, the new Christianity was in competition with the old Paganism. The Church saw that if they could convert the rulers of the kingdoms, and side with them, they could establish themselves in the country. Equally, the kings saw that the support of the Church would help to maintain their kingdoms. By the 9th century, anyone still practising pagan rituals was liable to marked as a witch or sorcerer, and could be executed.

"If any wicca, or wiglaer, or false swearer, or morthwyrtha, or any foul contaminated, manifest horcwenan(whore), be anywhere in the land, man shall drive them out."

Execution

Whatever their particular crime was, these three unfortunate people were sentenced to death. Hanging was the preferred method of execution, but it was quite normal to leave the bodies hanging in full view until they rotted and fell apart - a clear signal to others of the power of the law and justice, and a deterrent to others.

Anglo-Saxon poets described the awful fate of death by hanging.

One shall ride the high gallows and upon his death hang until his soul's treasury, his bloody bone – framed body, disintegrates. There the raven, black of plumage will pluck out the sight from his head and shred the soulless corpse - and he cannot fend off with his hands the loathsome bird of prey from its evil intent. His life is fled and deprived of his senses, beyond hope of survival, he suffers his lot, pallid upon the beam, enveloped in the midst of death. His name is damned. "*The Fortunes of Men*" - 10th century

The coming of the Vikings

The estate centre was abandoned, but the land was not left empty for long. Traces of shallow ditches were found, surrounding little paddocks and yards, and more postholes outlining rectangular houses. Over by the later main road, a sunken floored building was found, with a circular ditch nearby - which may have surrounded a hay rick as a defence against rats. The pottery from these remains is of a 9th to 10th century date - a time when this part of the country was controlled by new invaders - the Vikings.

Just as the three great kingdoms of Mercia, Wessex and Northumbria were beginning to settle into some sort of peaceful co-existence, their stability was rocked by the invaders from across the North Sea. The Vikings came from modern day Denmark - and in many ways their warlike and aggressive culture harked back to the early Saxon invaders of England. At first, content with hit-and-run raids on the east coast, the Vikings gradually became bolder and more confident, striking deeper and deeper into the heartlands of Mercia and Northumbria, and later Wessex as well. They struck at the monasteries for loot and the towns and villages for slaves. Those living near the east coast lived in constant danger of a sudden attack from "the Norsemen" - and longed for bad weather. One monk, while copying a manuscript

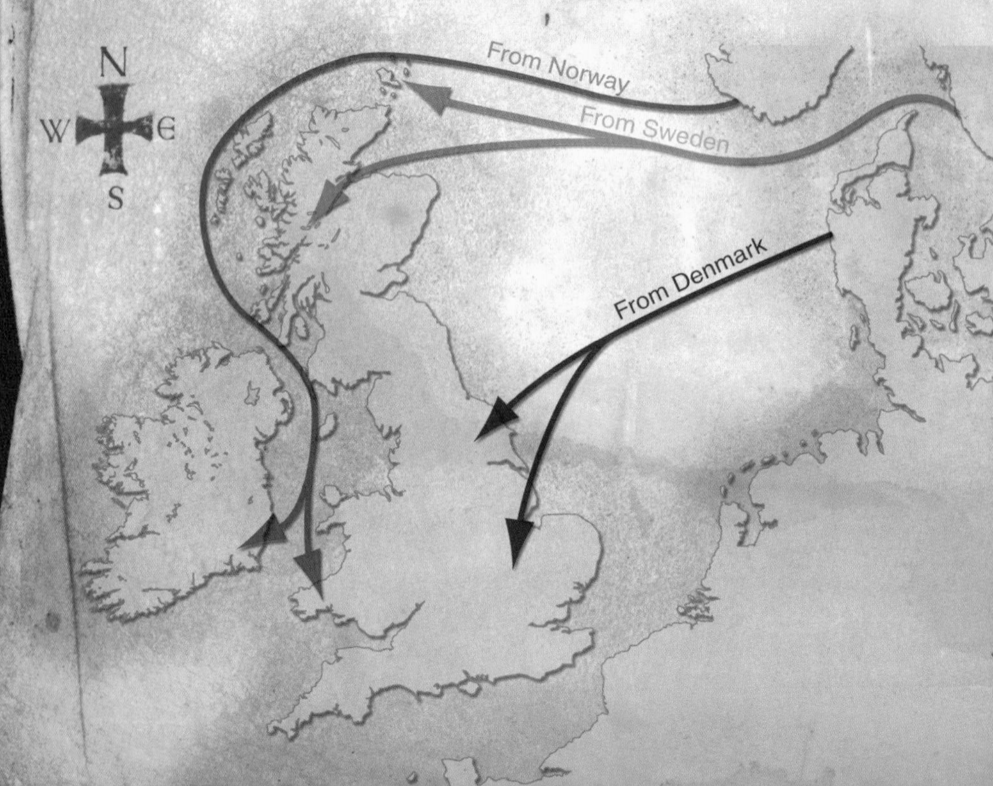

on a dark and stormy night, scribbled in the margin an ironic verse:

'Bitter and wild is the wind tonight
Tossing the tresses of the sea to white
On such a night as this I feel at ease
Fierce Norsemen only course the quiet seas'.

By the middle of the 9th century the Vikings had advanced deep inland, and controlled most of the eastern side of the country, including the area that would become Northamptonshire. It became known as the Danelaw. At Kings Meadow Lane, two finds (see above) hint at the years of Viking influence, one is a coin, struck in 891, the other a small piece of bronze sheet, no bigger then a fingernail, with a delicate design, called interlace, worked into one side. This sort of design is typical of Viking artwork, and the piece may have been part of a decorative plate fixed to a leather pouch.

When the Vikings were finally defeated and driven back by Alfred the Great, the Danelaw lands were reorganised into counties or shires - each with its own shire town. It may be that it was at this point that the modern core of Higham was established - with a market and a manor - and the Kings Meadow Lane area was left as a thinly populated relic of the old estate centre.

Children in Anglo-Saxon times

One more forlorn little grave was uncovered on the site. Some time in the 10th century a new born baby died, probably before it could be baptised. The church taught that a baby who died before baptism would

not reach heaven, and many believed that its spirit would return to trouble the living. A law from the 7th century gives us an idea how important it was to the newly Christian kings for their subject people to accept the new religion

'A child shall be baptised within 30 days. If this is not done, 30 shillings shall be paid in compensation. If it dies without being baptised, he* [the father] *shall pay everything he owns'

By the 10th century the scale of the penalty was reduced, but it was still severe. It seems that, in this case, the dead child was taken to a secluded spot just beyond the edge of the paddocks, and there hurriedly buried in a shallow grave - little more than a scoop in the ground.

How were children treated in Anglo-Saxon times?

Archaeology tells us little about how children were treated - it is in the laws and language of the Anglo-Saxons that we find clues. They had words for children (cild, bearn) and childish behaviour (cildisc, cildsung), words for children's clothes (cildcladas). Children's play was usually based around helping their parents, and it seems that childhood was seen as a time when a child learnt to be an adult. There was no specific age at which a child would actually be accepted as an adult, although early law codes define a legal 'adult' as someone of ten years or older. In their family or kin group the age of adulthood might be more varied - for a girl this would usually be the age at which she married, for a boy, the point when he could carry arms and stand alongside the warrior adult men. In both cases this point would usually be reached between 10 and 13 years of age.

HIGHAM FERRERS

Medieval Higham

By the time of the Norman Conquest in 1066 the centre of Higham was where it is today. Small excavations in the grounds of the later castle have found some pieces of Late Saxon pottery and traces of a timber building. Although the Saxon royal centre had long gone Higham was still important, as a manor held by Gytha, Countess of Hereford. By the time of Domesday, in 1086, the estate of Higham belonged to William Peverel, whose descendant later began work on the castle.

In 1155 Peverell forfeited Higham estate to King Henry II, who gave it to Robert Ferrers, Earl of Derby. It is from him that Higham became Higham Ferrers. In 1266 it was granted to Edmund Earl of Lancaster - becoming part of the Duchy of Lancaster. At the death of the last Duke of Lancaster, the Duchy - and its lands - were merged with the lands of the crown. From now on The Duchy and its lands, including Higham Ferrers, was run on behalf of the crown by a High Sheriff.

The Castle

Nothing remains today of the walls of the castle, but once it would have dominated the town. From eyewitness descriptions we know it consisted of an inner courtyard just north of the churchyard, and an outer yard, or bailey, further to the north. Both yards were surrounded by stone walls, topped with a wooden gallery. Within the inner yard were a wide range of buildings, including a Great Hall, the Lord's chamber, the Lady's Chamber, the Kitchen and associated buildings, store cellars, wine cellars and bakery. The manor farm occupied the outer yard. By the late 15th century the castle was in a very dilapidated state, and in 1523 it was finally demolished.

Chichele College

One of Higham Ferrers' most famous buildings, the College was founded in 1422 by Henry Chichele, Archbishop of Canterbury, whose family had long roots in Higham Ferrers. The college buildings were arranged around a closed courtyard - in the style of a medieval abbey. Today only the gatehouse, and the south range remains, although there are the foundations of other buildings still to see. Also founded in 1422 was the Bede House - a collegiate house to cater for 12 men and one woman.

The borough of Higham Ferrers

The 13th century was time of great prosperity in the land, and the fortunes of Higham reflect this. Many free boroughs were created at this time, as landowners realised that the promotion of town markets, and the creation of free boroughs and burgesses could bring investment, and profits.

In 1251 a Charter, witnessed by Henry III, granted free borough status to Higham Ferrers, and the rights of "burgage tenure" (the right to own property in the town) to 92 tenants (for a list of names see the inside back cover).

From the list of people we can find 16 trades recorded. These include 6 people involved in the preparation and sale of food (two butchers, baker, fishmonger, confectioner, cook); two leatherworkers (cobbler, skinner); two in clothes production (yarn maker, tailor); together with a smith, a miller and clerks. There were also three people apparently involved in agricultural activities (shepherd, horse keeper and swineherd).

The archaeology of Kings Meadow Lane at this time is meagre and low key. This part of town was now very much the outskirts. The curious remains of a cobbled courtyard, deep pits, and numerous stone-lined drains were found alongside the main north road. A few lengths of stone walls hint at quite a large dwelling - perhaps a farmhouse - but no clear evidence of a building. The Kings Meadow Lane area appeared to be sinking back into quiet farmland, but things were about to change in an unexpected way....

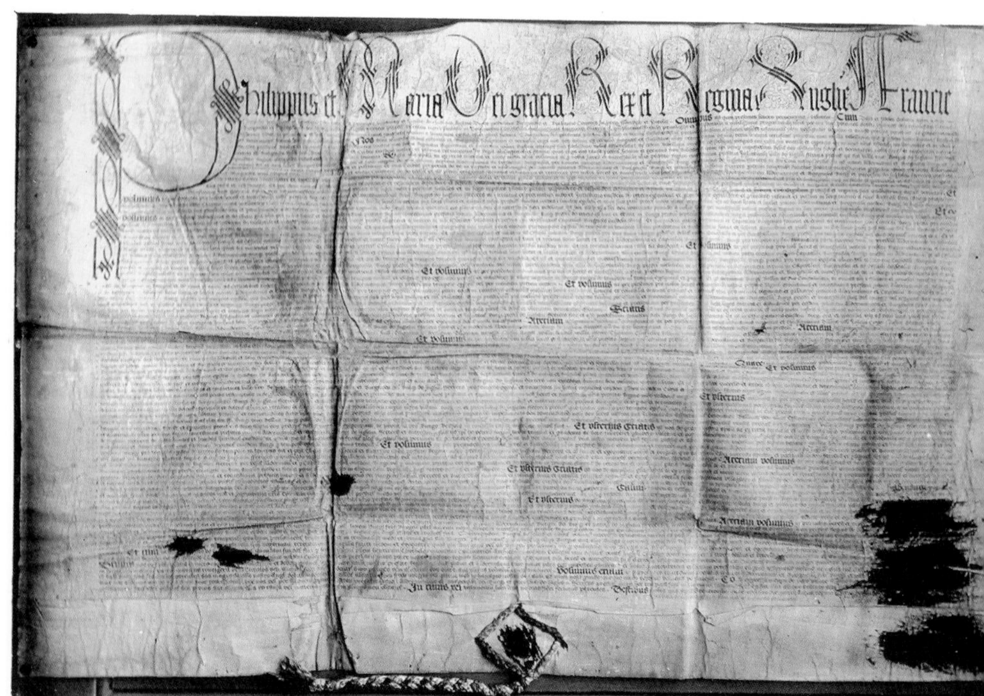
Philippus et Maria Dei gracia Rex et Regina Anglie Francie

William The Potter...

Pieces of pottery are one of the main kinds of evidence on an archaeological site. They can tell us when the site was occupied, what the people were doing, and how well-off they were.

But where did all this pottery come from? It was made in potters' workshops - medieval factories - dotted around the country. While we can often work out roughly where a type of pottery was made, it is rare to find the actual site where it was made. At Kings Meadow Lane we found three pottery kilns where a local type of pottery was made. One kiln contained nearly half a ton of broken pottery - rejects from the production line - there's no doubt that in the late 15th century this area was a veritable industrial estate!

"In 1436 William Potter bought a *messuage* in which croft there is a kiln for making pots and other earthen vessels"

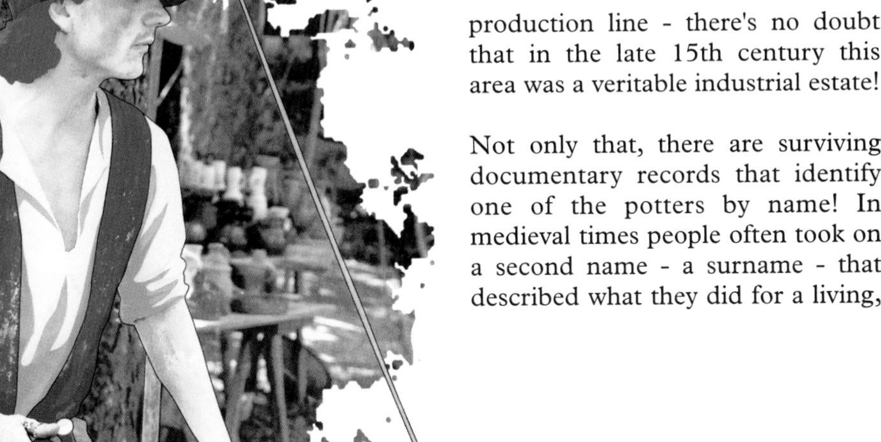

Not only that, there are surviving documentary records that identify one of the potters by name! In medieval times people often took on a second name - a surname - that described what they did for a living, so it is not surprising that the potter was called William Potter! (if you look at the list of people in the 1251 Charter on the inside back cover, you can work out the jobs of many of them by their names).

In 1436 William Potter bought a"messuage" - a plot of land - "in which croft there is a kiln for making pots and other earthen vessels". Thirty years later it is also recorded that he (or maybe his son) repaired an existing kiln on the site. Although these records tell us when William Potter was in business - it's worth getting a more scientific date to check if the kiln could have been one of his. On the large, well-preserved kiln, we tried archaeomagnetic dating, (for an explanation of this see page 47) which tells us when the kiln was last used. The date recorded was between 1385 and 1435, so this particular kiln was probably the one that William Potter bought.

What did a medieval pottery look like?

There would be a workshop with a wheel, to produce the pots, a drying shed, where the newly-made pots were laid out to dry, and a kiln, to fire the pots. By one of the kilns at Kings Meadow Lane the corner of the potters workshop was uncovered, alongside a cobblestone yard where the pots would have stood to dry.

The kiln itself could be of various sizes, and shapes - at Higham it consisted of a large central pit which contained a flat-topped platform. The inside of the pit was coated with clay, and the finger marks of the kiln maker were still visible on the clay. Each end of the pit narrowed to a funnel, leading to a stoke hole. Over the central pit there would have been a large dome built of clay, with a chimney hole in the

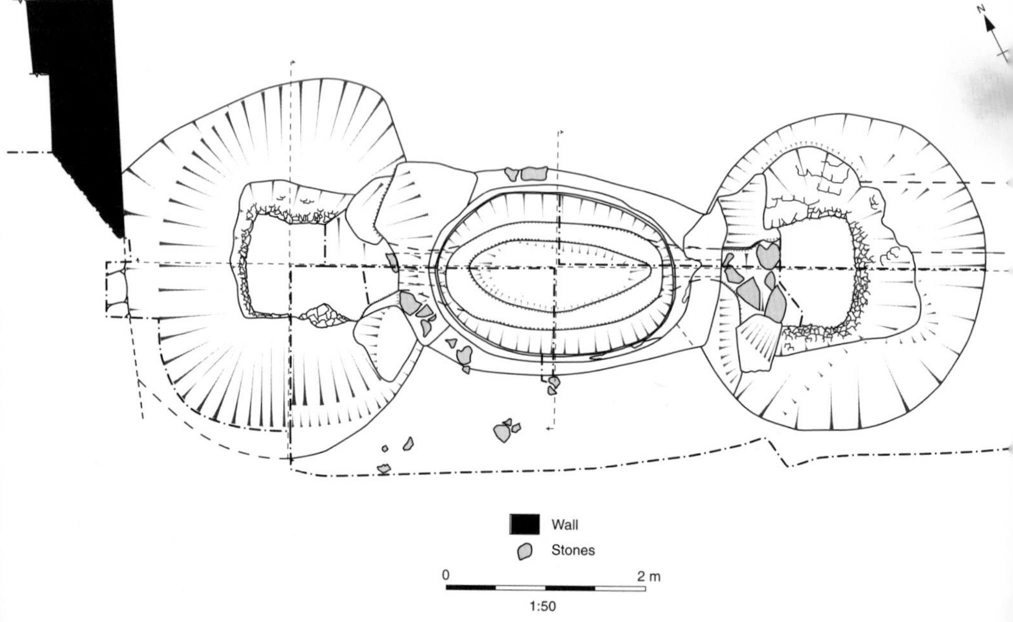

top. The newly made pots would be stacked on the platform inside the dome, and fires lit in the stokeholes. The fires would be fed with light brushwood - charred remains of thorny brushwood were found near the kiln. The hot air from the fire would be drawn up through the dome and, over a few days the intense heat would 'fire' the pots to a dark grey colour. The finished pots would be sold around the local countryside by peddlers, the travelling salesmen of their day!

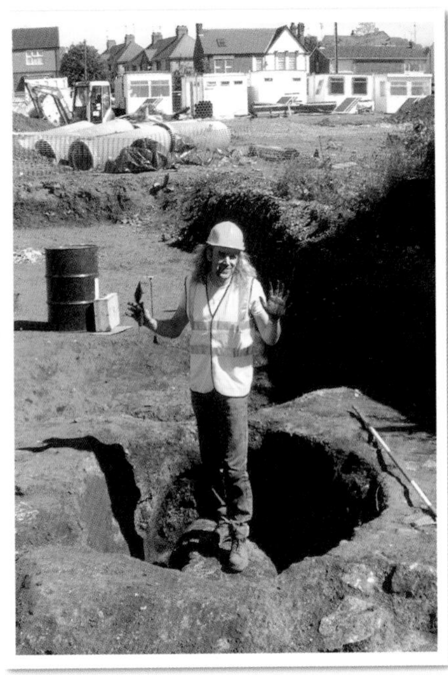

Pottery-making was an arduous and dirty job, which did not pay very well, and by the late 15th century potters were not considered high-class craftsmen - most potters were also farmers to supplement their income. Wherever possible their production sites were set away from the centre of town, as is the case at Higham Ferrers.

THE SPECIALIST'S REPORT

Paul Blinkhorn *Pottery Specialist*

The pots William Potter produced are a type known by archaeologists as Late Medieval Reduced Ware, a type common in this part of the country in the later 14th - 15th centuries. It is so-called because to achieve the uniform grey colour, the pots had to be fired in a tightly-sealed kiln with little oxygen present, which potters refer to as a 'reducing' atmosphere. The pots are well-made but quite coarse, with the large amounts of sand in the clay, giving the surfaces a rough feel, and they are almost entirely undecorated.

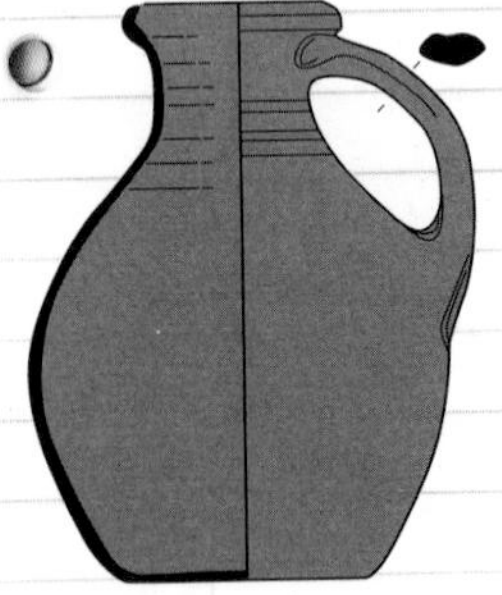

Large Jug

The pots were not glazed, despite the technique being common on other types of pottery at the time, and this probably means that William was making pottery designed to be cheap yet functional.

Only a small range of different types of pot were offered; pancheons, or large bowls, which had numerous uses in the medieval household; large jugs, carrying or storing water and other liquids; jars, another vessel type which had numerous functions, and bunghole cisterns. These were fat jugs for storing beer, with a hole in the side near the bottom from which the liquid could be poured. The hole would be plugged with a wooden peg. These cisterns became common as the home-brewing of beer became widespread during the 14th century,

Dripping pan

A small number of specialist cooking vessels, known as dripping pans, were also found. These would have been placed under spit-roasting meat to catch the dripping fat, which could then be used for the making of sauces and gravy.

HIGHAM FERRERS

Roads

The changing character of a settlement can often be shown by the road network and how it changes. Today Kings Meadow Lane is little more than a footpath - and yet it was once the most important road in the area!

The excavation found evidence of a Roman track leading down from the high ground to the river. This later evolved into the principal road from the tribute centre across to the Saxon royal centre at Irthlingborough.

However, there were also signs that a lesser track led north - past the horseshoe enclosure and onwards to Raunds and Stanwick.

With the closure of the Saxon royal centre the importance of the lane declined, and the new bridge built by the Abbot of Peterborough in 1227 meant that most traffic now went north out of the town instead of northwest. Such building as took place was close to the new main road, not the dead end of Kings Meadow Lane.

How did the Lane get its name?

We do not know for sure. At some point, probably after the Duchy of Lancaster's lands became the property of the King, a meadow on the Irthlingborough side of the River Nene became known as Kings Meadow. The lane that ran from Higham Ferrers across the river and past the meadow became known as Kings Meadow Lane.
But names change, often to suit their changing purpose - for much of the past 100 years it has been known as Lover's Lane!

Back to the country - and on foot to the future

By the late 17th century Higham Ferrers was pale shadow of its former self. Chichele College and the castle were no more, and it had lost the right to hold the corn market to its rival Wellingborough. More people were leaving the town than staying. In 1712 Higham Ferrers was dismissed as ***"small and not very populous"*** in a description by antiquary J. Morton.

The town had shrunk, and Kings Meadow Lane now ran through agricultural fields. What had once been part of a Saxon royal centre, and later an industrial estate was now open field and waste ground. For a time a windmill occupied the top of the hill, by the main road, and gave its name to modern Windmill Banks.

The archaeologists found evidence - in the form of the foundations and back yards, of little cottages - at the top of the Lane - later to be called Walnut Tree Green, and along the main road north. The land behind, now called Townend Furlong, was divided up into strip fields, and cultivated in the ridge-and-furrow style. This meant that fields were divided into thin strips. The method of ploughing each strip meant that the soil was gradually moved to the centre of the strip, leaving a wide, shallow ditch along each side. We found some of those wide, shallow ditches, and they match the layout of the strip fields on the old maps of the area (see over page).

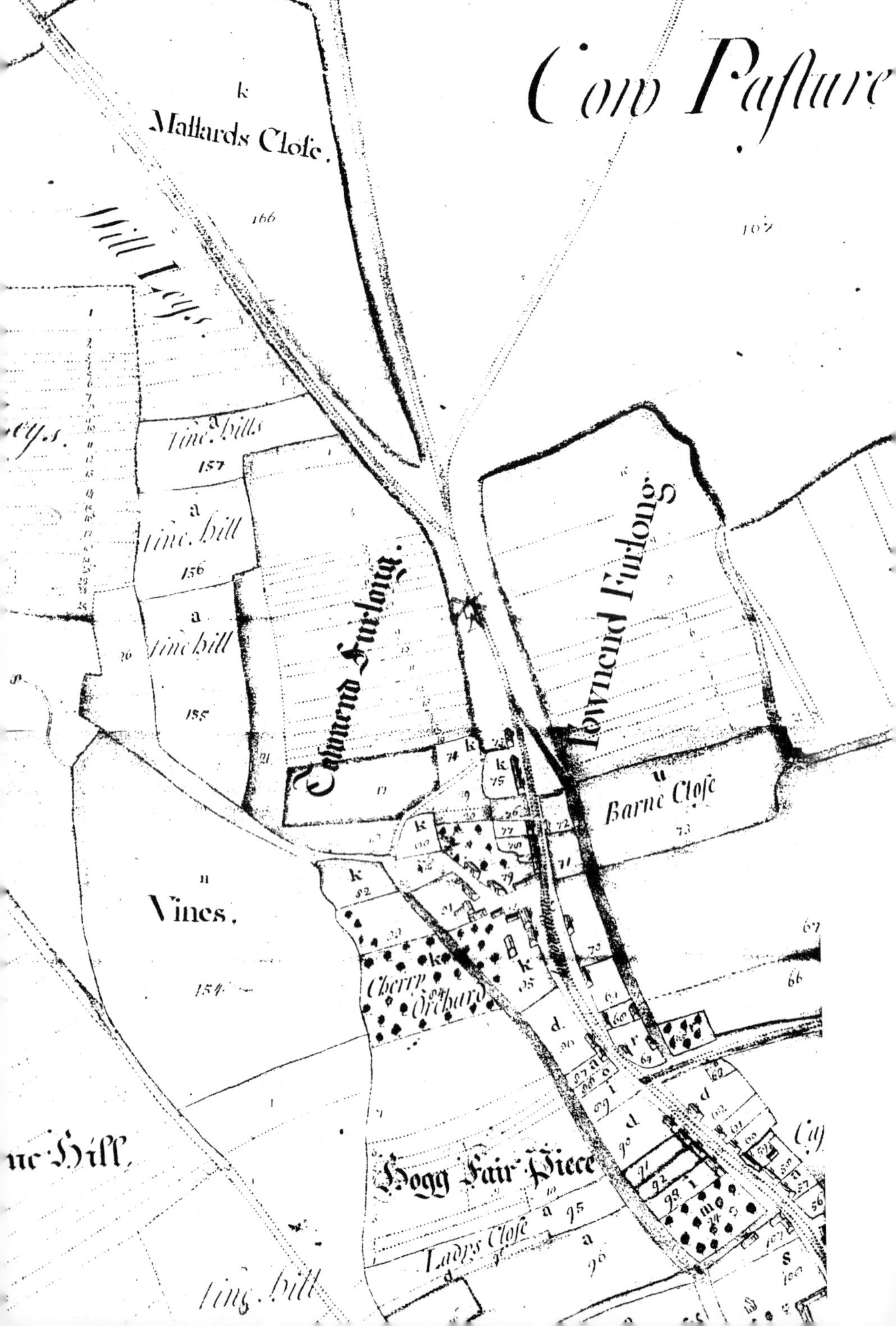

Cow Pasture
Mallards Close
Mill Leys
Vine hills
Vine hill
Townend Furlong
Townend Furlong
Barne Close
Vines
Cherry Orchard
Hogg Fair Piece
Ladys Close
ne Hill
Vine hill

Excavation– Before During & After...

There is great deal that can be learned about a site before the diggers get to work. These techniques can save much expensive digging, and wasted effort.

Aerial photography

Where ditches have been dug in the past, and filled in with soil, their lines will show as darker colours in the modern crops growing over them, as the deeper soil holds more water, and the crops grow taller and ripen later. It was by this means that the great horseshoe enclosure was noticed.

Fieldwalking

By systematically searching for pottery and other finds over recently ploughed land, a plan can be made to show where there are concentrations of finds, and therefore probable occupation sites. The concentrations of early and middle Saxon pottery showed clear differences when set against the line of the horseshoe enclosure

Geophysical survey

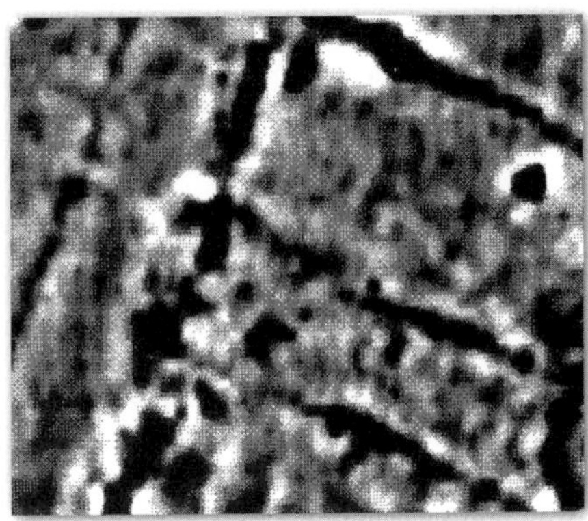

Buried pits, ditches and sites of burning can be traced by a magnetometer survey, which detects the disturbed magnetic fields of these features, and reproduces the results as a map.

Stratigraphy

An excavation is never about just finding things for the sake of it. It is about the events that happened, the order in which they happened, and

why they happened.

One of the most important questions that an excavation has to answer is: `In what order did these events happen?' If we can answer this we can tell how a site developed. Let us suppose that a ditch or pit is dug, and used, and eventually is filled in, or fills in naturally. If another ditch or pit is then dug that cuts into the earlier filled-in one, this can be seen during excavation, and the order of events - the stratigraphy - recorded.

What happens if there isn't any stratigraphy?

On sites where few features cut each other, working out a sequence of events is much more difficult, and relies upon the dating evidence that might be found in the fill of the pit or ditch, and also on the feature's position in relation to others

What is dating evidence?

This is where the objects help us. Pottery types and styles can tell us when a pit or ditch was in use, and other objects such as jewelry, coins, and tools, can also help. Recently, two methods have been developed to give us scientific dating.

Archaeomagnetic dating

Heating rock or clay to a very high temperature - for instance in a kiln - fixes the direction of its magnetic field to that of the earth. The earth's magnetic pole has always wandered over time. So if we can match the direction of the kiln's magnetic field to a point in the past when the earth's magnetic field had the same direction, we can tell - within a margin of years - when the kiln was in use.

Radiocarbon dating

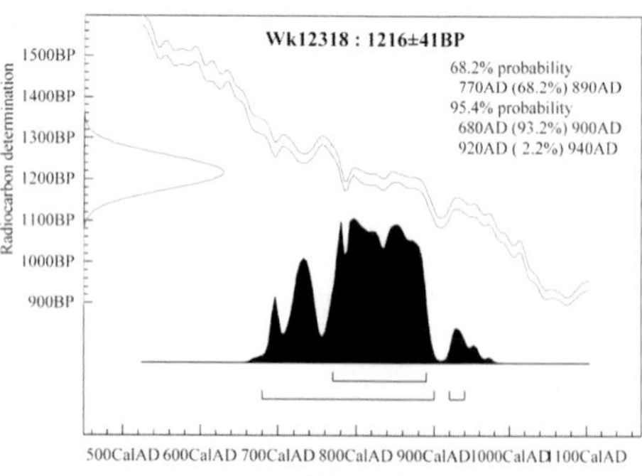

All living things absorb an isotope of Carbon - C14 - from the atmosphere. After death the amount of C14 they have absorbed starts to decline. The 'half-life' of Carbon 14 is known to be 5,730 years - that is, after that time half the C14 will have decayed, so if the C14 in an object that was once alive is measured, its age, within a margin of years - can be calculated. The result can be displayed as a chart - the width of the black shape shows the date range, and the tallest part shows the most probable date within that range.

Afterwards...

If the excavation gives us evidence about the past, then post-excavation tries to turn that evidence into understanding.

All the different categories of evidence are analysed by specialists. Pottery, animal bone, human bone, plant remains, metal objects - comparisons are made with what is already known from other sites. Are they similar? In what ways are they different, and why might that be?

The real skill of the archaeologist is to interpret the evidence to get as close to what happened as possible. It is almost never the case that we can explain exactly what events happened at a point in the past and why. At best we can say what the evidence probably means.

Full circle

New homes, along with a new school, now cover the land on either side of Kings Meadow Lane. Hundreds of new settlers have moved in - like those first English 1500 years ago - each with their own culture, their own beliefs, eager to add to the life of the community of Higham Ferrers.

Where new homes now stand there were the new homes of the first English.

Where now winds a leafy footpath, there once was a royal centre of the most powerful kingdom in the land - a centre of authority and ruthless justice.

Where now lie new gardens - there once was a bustling medieval factory.

Only by the making of these new homes has the story of their predecessors and the origins of the community itself come to light. The story doesn't end here - today's new homes are tomorrow's archaeology.

The cycle continues.....

A 45
Site 9
THE ROMAN
SMALL TOWN
Site 10

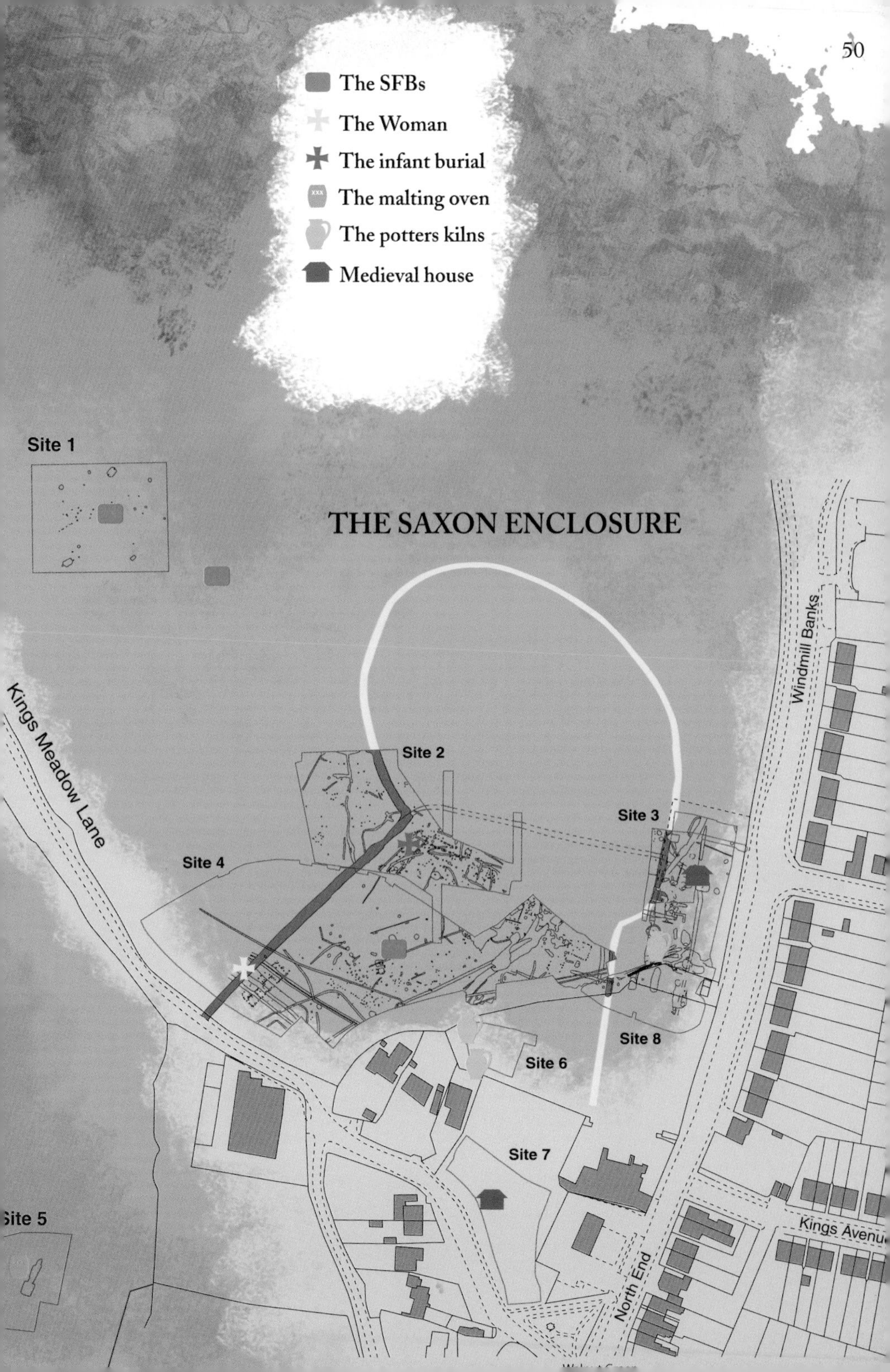
The SFBs
The Woman
The infant burial
The malting oven
The potters kilns
Medieval house
THE SAXON ENCLOSURE
Site 1
Site 2
Site 3
Site 4
Site 5
Site 6
Site 7
Site 8
Kings Meadow Lane
Windmill Banks
North End
Kings Avenue

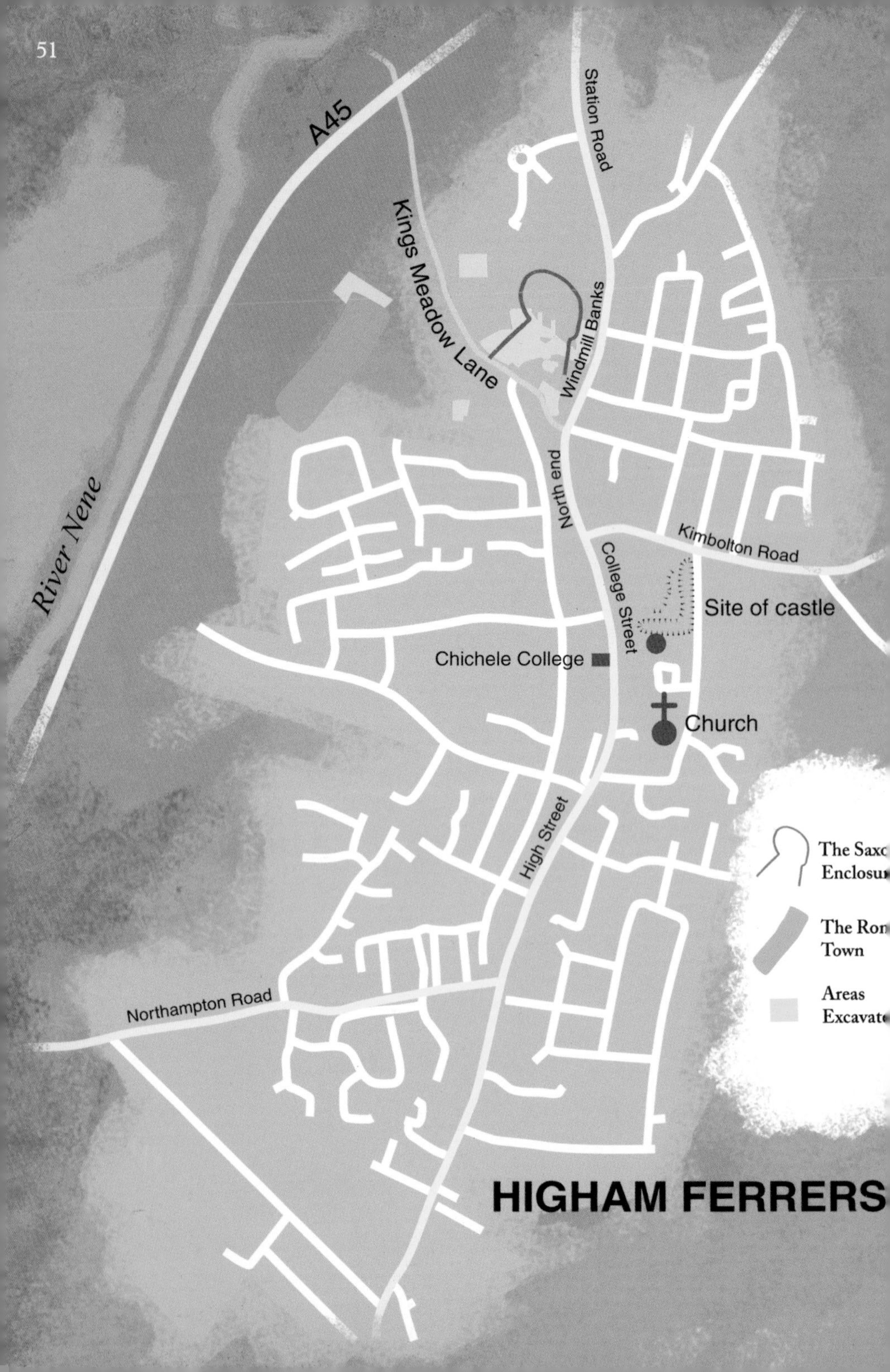

A45

Station Road

Kings Meadow Lane

Windmill Banks

River Nene

North end

Kimbolton Road

College Street

Site of castle

Chichele College

Church

High Street

Northampton Road

The Saxo
Enclosur

The Ron
Town

Areas
Excavate

HIGHAM FERRERS